Christmas Tree Farm

BY DAVID BUDBILL
ILLUSTRATED BY DONALD CARRICK

Macmillan Publishing Co., Inc.
New York
Collier Macmillan Publishers
London

2   3   4   5   6   7   8   9   10

The four-color illustrations were prepared as black pencil and wash
drawings with overlays for red, yellow and blue. The typeface is
Alphatype Atlantic, with the display set in Americana.

Library of Congress Cataloging in Publication Data
Budbill, David.   Christmas tree farm.
1. Christmas trees — Juvenile literature.   2. Tree farms — Vermont —
Juvenile literature.   [1. Christmas trees.   2. Tree farms]
I. Carrick, Donald, illus.   II. Title.
SB437.5.C6B8   634.9'75   73-6051   ISBN 0-02-715330-4

for the crew
maudit sapin!

Far to the north, when the snow is almost gone, Marcel and the other workers go into the woods and gently pull tiny evergreen trees out of the wet moss.

They take the trees to an open field and plant them in long rows. Spring begins this way for Marcel and the other men. They are Christmas tree farmers.

When the planting is done, Marcel and the men work among the bigger, older trees. They walk up and down the rows, giving each tree a handful of fertilizer. The fertilizer will feed the trees, helping them grow bushy and green.

After the morning's work, it is good to rest at noon and eat sandwiches in the warm spring sun. The men listen to Marcel tell stories. The men don't see them, but not far away a curious mother deer and her fawn are watching.

When summer comes, the men mow between the rows of trees, cutting the briars and ferns so the trees will have light and room to grow. Where the hills are too steep for mowers, other men cut the weeds with brush saws.

By the time the mowing is done, the short northern summer
is almost gone. Because the days are colder now, the Christmas
trees have stopped growing. It is time to shape the trees.
The men use pruning poles to trim their branches.

Fall is harvest time. The men who sell trees in the cities have sent Marcel their orders. Marcel walks up and down the rows of trees tagging the ones he wants to cut, some large ones, some small ones, some in between.

Then Marcel cuts the trees with a chain saw while others drag

the fallen trees to large piles along the woods road.

A tractor comes to the woods pulling a machine. The men push the trees into the machine and when they come out the other side they are wrapped tightly in a net to protect their branches. The netting makes the trees easier to handle and helps keep them fresh until they reach the city.

The wrapped trees are loaded onto trucks and hauled out of the woods. At the farmhouse yard they are stacked according to size.

It snows almost every day now.

The first big truck arrives. It takes all day to load the truck.

When the trees are loaded, the men wave good-by

as the truck pulls away from the farm and heads

down the mountain toward the city.

Weeks later, after the last truck has been loaded, work on the Christmas tree farm is done for another year. Marcel says good-by to the men and takes his own tree home.

Outdoors on the quiet mountainside, the Christmas trees of years

to come stand in the snow as winter deepens around them.

DATE DUE

JAN 0 5 2001